When Loved ones Die

Coping with loss

Timothy White, Sr.

For information contact:
info@uptownmediaventures.com

Book and Cover design by Tim White Publishing

ISBN: 978-1-68121-111-4

10 9 8 7 6 5 4 3 2 1

Table of Contents

Prologue

What happens when those we love and care about most die? What affect does it have on those who are left behind? Why do we feel so out of place and hurt even with the belief that our loved one is in a better place?

Why does death seem to come at the most inopportune time? Most people think of death as if it is some far away "thing", and that it should not happen to babies or children, or that it should only take place when we become old and are full of days.

Unfortunately, the harsh reality is this; we don't prepare for death as much as we prepare for life. And live our lives as if we will never die.

One of the greatest difficulties facing human beings is that of death, and many of us are trying various methods to remain youthful looking. But doing this does nothing to prevent death or cause us to live longer. We don't truly understand life, so it's very difficult to reconcile the ending of life physically as we have come to know it.

We're born knowing only life, but as we grow, we begin to see death all around us. We come into the world on a journey of discovery, but we come also with a time stamp, or expiration date as well.

Death is unfamiliar to us, it does not come with a manual on what to expect or even when to expect it. In the process of time and often first-hand experience is where we begin questioning death, and what takes place with every living thing.

Death brings a release to some, and sorrow to others; it's seen as both good and evil. It can be subtle, and can be violent, it is light and dark, and it can be a friend or an enemy.

As certain as there's life there's death, and it stands as close to us as life, even walking with us every day of our lives with many of us unaware how close it is.

Death is the one single occurrence that as human beings we do not put much thought into. We see it occur in the lives of people around us, but rarely think of it as something that will come to our homes, or our loved ones. Death does not play favorites, and it does not matter the status, the location or the power of the individual, death will reach out and touch everyone, the question again becomes are we prepared for it?

Some say it's morbid to think about death or about when it could occur, but the truth is, each of us as surely as we live we will die, and there are those who have departed before us in death young and old letting us know it's coming for each of us.

Some people live with the faith they are only transitioning to a more glorious place, while others say it matters little to them where they are going, if they are going anywhere at all once, they die.

We hope to shed a little light on the matter of death and how it affects all of us on various levels. As you continue through this book it's my prayer that hopefully you gain a greater understanding as you do of death and how we as believers should respond to the loss of loved ones.

The bible is filled with death from beginning to end; it's spoken of extensively throughout scripture. We are introduced to death first in Genesis and culminating with its destruction in the book of Revelation.

How death affects us is different for everyone depending on the individual, and the closeness of the people who are involved. We talk about life, but seldom do we speak of death, as if it's taboo to speak of it, or will never happen to us.

The bible is filled with literally thousands of deaths, and we will examine a few of them in the hope of shedding some measure of light on this matter of death and dying.

Each of us is born learning life and having never died to know what is waiting for us on the other side. Of course, there are those who say they have traveled to the other side by what they call near death experiences, I'm not here to debate what they believe or even if these things they say are true. I will give what the word of God says and teaches, and let you make up your own mind what you choose to believe.

Weeping may endure for a night, but joy comes in the morning (Psalms.30: 5), this is a scripture said to give comfort to those who suffer adversity, death is inescapable. Death can be found all around us, but it carries no real meaning until it strikes in our lives and homes. Death is not something the average person prepares for, even with the knowledge that it cannot be escaped or avoided.

Death becomes tragic to many of us because we are so ill prepared for it. As seekers of pleasure we don't think about death, it always seems far away, so when it does come it seems to catch us off guard and brings with it, times of overwhelming sadness.

Death is an enemy to some, it's seen as a friend to certain ones, while others fear it. There are those who see death as a welcome release from the physical or mental issues they face in life. Death is very one sided, meaning we try to understand it from life's side or perspective.

There was no one who could shed a true light on death, it's limits, or its power, that is not until Jesus Christ came along.

Christ is the only person we know of that came into the world and died (*for three days*) and rose again proclaiming, he had **the key to Hell and death** (Revelations.1: 18).

Jesus Christ had accomplished the impossible. He died and came back from the dead, to let us know by example, that death no longer has power over us, and that there is life, a new life after we transition from this one, in Him.

I hope you will take your time and read carefully what is written in the pages of this book. But it is my greater hope that you apply the simple truths as related here concerning how we should deal with death, and cope with the loss of loved ones brought about by it.

Why Me?

The loss of a love one can be one of the most difficult and painful times in an individual's life. Each of us understands life has a beginning and a conclusion, even if we are not willing to think about it.

Over the years I have spoken and had the opportunity to share with many people who had suffered the loss of a family member, some told me they were angry with God and they did not feel they were wrong for how they felt saying, why would God take their loved one away, and how they believed this was not fair to them?

Most people blame God for how they feel and believe he is unjust by taking their loved one away from them. As human beings we can be very selfish, we think of ourselves first and foremost. It was some years ago I was in a conversation with an older Christian woman, Amy (not her real name) who was angry with God for taking her son away from her and she was not ashamed to let her feelings be known to others. Amy sat and tears would begin to fill her eyes as she shared her story, as well as her love for her son whose life was senselessly taken away from him as she explained, and why would God take her only son away from her leaving her all alone?

Why would a loving God take her son away from her, he was all she had in this world and she could not understand why God would allow her to hurt so much.

Scripture is far easier to quote than it is to apply, as she continued to talk I could feel the pain in her voice as she expressed her doubts, how could God allow her to remain in such pain year after year she wondered aloud, she was not the first person to feel this way but one of the few who I found willing to express it openly.

Was God wrong in taking her son away from her as she believed, or was there a greater plan for her life being worked out that she was not willing, or possibly unable to see?

The bible teaches us that all things work together for good to them that love God, those who are the called according to his purpose (Romans.8: 28).

The question becomes how the death of her son could be good. Death when it hits home becomes an unacceptable reality and all too often, we find ourselves blaming God for not preventing it in the first place.

During the course of our conversation which was lengthy I listened carefully to what she had to share with me about the loss she felt was tragic, but then Amy asked me what did I think about what she said, and was she wrong in feeling the way she did? (*Most people don't ask questions seeking the truth but only to have someone commiserate with them*).

I'm a firm believer that you should never ask questions that you really don't want to know the answer to, Amy said she valued my opinion and would like to know what I thought as a Christian. The truth is not always easy to hear but the truth will make people free, but it also challenges thinking and perception of things when we step away from the emotional attachments we have to a particular event or experience.

The questions asked most by believers and non-believers alike are, **"why me"**, **"why did this have to happen to me"**, and **"what did I do wrong"**.

When we are confronted with death's reality we are rarely prepared for it, and if the unthinkable happens and we lose a loved one to murder, in our anguish we seek answers from God or we blame him for not preventing it in the first place.

When we feel we are unable to cope with our loss we then affix blame either to ourselves or others for what has taken place. For example, when a loved one is lost due to violence, particularly children, as parents we put on guilt first, questioning our parenting or in a friendship our loyalty for possibly bringing about this tragedy in some way, comments like, they "**would've** still been here if I", "I **should've** seen the signs", "I **could've** been a better friend, listener, or parent".

As you continue to read you will find that it has nothing to do with being in the wrong place at the right time, or the right place at the wrong time, each of us has an appointment with death, it's inescapable and unavoidable.

The unfortunate side of death is this; we can put ourselves in a position of danger that could possibly lead to ours, or someone else's death. For example in the bible there were three young men (Hananiah, Mishael, and Azariah), who refused to obey the Kings (Nebuchadnezzar's) degree to WORSHIP the image he had built, he commanded that at the sound of music playing everyone was to worship his image (Daniel.3: 3-6), their actions would have a direct effect on themselves and others because of the decision they made because of faith, and their faith was leading them to the flames of the kings fiery furnace.

Shadrach, Meshach, and Abednego faced certain death because they embraced their faith and not fear, they were ready to die for God rather than fall captive spiritually to man and his devices, and it was jealousy that led those in positions of power to go after these three men of God (Daniel.3: 12-25).

Later we would find something similar as those who were envious and jealous of Daniel sought to have him put to death because he was a man of prayer (Daniel.6:1-23).

Even as Shadrach, Meshach, and Abednego survived their ordeal, those who threw them into the furnace were slain and those who accused Daniel were also slain and their families for the things they sought to do to Daniel, apparently it was a conspiracy that all of their family members were privy to, and their evil actions brought about the death of others as we will see again later.

We might not ever get over our loss of loved ones, but it's possible to get through it, **if we give ourselves permission to do so** and trust the Lord to carry us through our time of trial.

Death is an inescapable fact of life that each of us will have to deal with one day; the missing factor is when this will take place, and what the response will be. God can deliver us in life or in death according to his will.

The three Hebrew boys had no idea they would be called upon to act on their faith in such a dramatic way, nor did Daniel have any idea how his faith would be tested, it was an unknown, and Daniel had no idea what would happen from day to day, but he trusted God and moved by his faith.

The Christian sister Amy, I had been listening to had in the years following her son's death, had been building **a wall of doubt** around her faith, and in the course of time was seeking to have someone accept her views concerning her anger, and displeasure with God, and justify her feelings.

Was she right to feel the way she did, in her mind she was, and even for a moment (emotionally speaking) **we might** blame God, but this should not translate into years of resentment?

Let's go back to the Garden of Eden and look at what took place when Man sinned, and when God questioned Eve about her sin, (act of disobedience), she without hesitation immediately placed blame on the serpent. When the Lord God questioned Adam, he blamed God (Genesis.3: 1-13).

It's natural for us almost automatically to blame God when things go wrong in our lives, even for the things we bring on ourselves. Death is the result of man's original sin in the Garden and is now passed on to every generation.

Had this mom, Amy, done anything personally that could have brought about the death of her son, was her son in the wrong place at the wrong time as some had suggested to her. In every death that occurs, those who get information pertaining to it often become either a witness for the prosecution or the defense, assuming to know the truth, though unknown, they attempt to determine what took place, and who should be punished for the loss experienced, without knowledge of what could have actually taken place.

How many times have you asked the question "why me" in your life as if you were better than the circumstance confronting you? Another question that should be asked immediately is "why not you"? For some reason we allow ourselves to believe we are better than others in life and that tragedy should not befall us, our homes or families.

Hear the words of Jesus when he gave this very simple truth, God makes the sun to rise on the evil and the good and sends his rain (*judgment, compassion*) on the just and unjust (Matthew.5: 45). Was this a complex or confusing statement, absolutely not, in fact it's very clear what Jesus is saying, should only good things happen to you because you are a follower of good, and should evil only follow those who do evil, let's remember that God is creator of both?

When there's rain the rain does not choose to only fall on those who are evil, a flood does not go around the house of those who are believers washing away only the homes of evil people, those who are evil rise up in the morning just as those who are good. Lives lost are not only of those who do not know the Lord. God is not a respecter of persons (Acts.10: 34), it does not matter who we are, or think we are, death will come for us.

History has shown us that so-called good people die; they are not immune to it. When God sent Moses to Pharaoh with the message to let his people go the last act before their release was a plague in the form of death, the death of all the firstborn, it's here that we can see the practical side of what Jesus said in the New Testament of it raining on the just as well as the unjust.

The Israelites were instructed what to do in order for their firstborn to escape the death plague to come, the death angel would come to every household, regardless of who was inside, and would claim the life of the firstborn child, if they did not do what the Lord had commanded for the death angel to pass over their house.

God was not going to send the death angel only to the homes of Egyptians, but he would come to all homes, the difference is obedience, and being obedient to what God said to do.

God was not picking on any one group of people, he's a just God, but it was the sins of Egypt that the Lord was dealing with, God does not hate the sinner but the sin.

God loved the world so much that he sent his Son, (Christ) to open the door to Heaven to allow anyone and everyone who would believe in him, in and they would not perish but have everlasting life. (Read John.3: 16; 3: 36).

God's love is from everlasting to everlasting and his mercy endures forever, and he promised he would never leave us or forsake us. So, in the midst of our pain He is there with us. As we ask the question why me, the answer becomes clear when we lean and depend on the Lord for his strength and guidance in our times of loss.

The Living and The Dead

Two angels at the tomb of Jesus asked a very powerful question to the disciples who came to the tomb to complete the burial process that could not be finished because of the Sabbath, part of the Law that restricted certain kinds of work (Exodus.20: 9, 10), they sought to complete the ritual for their dead friend Jesus, they thought might be their promised messiah.

The question asked: **why seek ye the living among the dead** (Luke.24: 5)? How do you answer such a question as this, what explanation is there for the living to go visiting the place of the dead?

The living part of man is his soul and spirit, both are housed in a fleshly body, and we know these bodies we carry are temporary, and one day will go back to the dust they were created from (Genesis.3: 19), and because of man's sinful nature, sin is passed on from generation to generation being accompanied by death.

As saints we thank God for the finished work of Christ, it was his dying on the cross that brought us freedom from the penalty of sin, giving us power over sin and ultimately to take us one day, even from the very presence of sin. But until that day, we have to understand that death will continue.

The hope of eternal life is found in our faith in the words of Jesus Christ, and his example, trusting in the Lord with all our hearts that the things written are faithful and true.

In the opening words of this chapter we read 8 words spoken by an angel questioning the actions of those who came to the grave of Jesus, "WHY SEEK YE THE LIVING AMONG THE DEAD"?

It was a gentle reprimand to them for their lack of faith. Many of them were aware of the doctrine (teaching) of Jesus, how he went about feeding the hungry, healing the sick, giving sight to the blind and even raising the dead. Some amazing miracles performed by Jesus for others, but what about Jesus himself? They saw him arrested, scourged, beat and nailed to a cross.

Jesus the healer of the nation hangs on a cross and did nothing to save himself, they watched him suffer and cry out to God, and they saw him take his last breath and die.

What happened? Everyone saw Jesus as just another prophet, a godly man, yes, but still just a man, and like all men before him Jesus also died.

Jesus taught like no others before him and was even compared to a few of them (Matthew16: 13, 14), but Jesus was dead also, like all those who came before him.

Jesus was buried in a hurry and the disciples going to the grave did so with intentions of completing the embalming process and mourn for their slain teacher. This act was not necessary, because it was already done by Mary when she poured the ointment on his feet and wipe his feet with her hair (Mark.14:1-8).

Jesus' words that he would raise again after three days fell on deaf ears, they focused on the ritual of the dead, and not on the words Christ had spoken concerning his death and resurrection. So, it's no wonder why the angels reprimanded them for their lack of faith.

Why do we spend millions of dollars on grave sites and flowers, and go to cemeteries and weep for loved ones even talking to the headstones of those who are not in the shells left behind, going to where the dead are is not where we find life?

The angel's question to those at Jesus' grave was one for the ages. Why are you looking for the living among the dead?

In other words, the angels were saying to them, if they believed what Jesus said they would not be there. **But it wasn't that they did not have faith, it**

was just a weak and frightened faith. They had to be reminded of what Jesus said (Luke.24: 8).

What about you and I, as we look at early disciples and their shortcomings, can we see our own as well? When there is a death do we become forgetful of what the word of God tells us to do as well?

Death, if we are not careful can blind us, it can close our spiritual eyes of faith, and we can find ourselves walking according to our flesh. Saying and doing things we should not. Had they thought about the words of Jesus, maybe they would have understood what he meant. Jesus promised them that he would raise from the dead on the third day (Luke.24: 7;18: 31-33), it was now three days since Jesus' death when they were heading to his tomb to give Jesus a decent burial.

Sadly, the grief we experience with the loss of a loved one can be found overshadowing our faith, and we miss seeing what the Lord has set before us.

Mary of Magdala assumed the resurrected Jesus was a gardener who might have taken his body away to an undisclosed place (John.20: 11-15), these were not the words or actions of a woman who believed Jesus had risen from the dead.

The Pharisees sought to prevent what they thought would be grave robbing, and perpetrating a resurrection hoax, by having Pilate post guards on the tomb of Christ (Matthew.27:62-66) effectively hoping to prevent the disciples, or anyone for that matter from stilling his body.

So, what happened **at Jesus' tomb**, I suppose a better question would be what happened **in Jesus' tomb**?

The body of Jesus lay inside a tomb that was never used before (Luke.23.50-53; John.19: 38-42), the tomb was sealed, and guards posted on the outside, no one was getting in or out, at least that was the plan.

The angels (messengers) were sent to upbraid the disciples for their lack of faith, saying in effect "what are you doing here; do you think to find the living among the dead"?

Certainly, it was difficult for these disciples to believe that after all Jesus was put through three days earlier by torture, there was any way humanly possible he might possibly be alive. Jesus' death was brutal and violent, and the disciple's attention was focused on death, not life.

The living do not cohabitate with the dead, the dead do not offer the living comfort, peace or joy. The living and the dead have nothing in common.

When things appear to be hopeless is the time when God works wonders. Death could not bind Christ who is our hope, and the first fruit of those who are raised from the dead, the empty tomb is a reminder to you and I that there is a greater life waiting for all those who have put their trust in Christ. The tomb was left open for all to look inside and know that death no longer has power, and that there is life after death, and the dead do rise.

The Apostle Paul said, I am crucified (died) with Christ nevertheless I live (I'm alive), yet not I (the dead person), but Christ lives in me (the living saint) and the life I now live (raised from spiritual death) in the flesh, I live by faith in the Son of God who loved me died and gave himself for me (Galatians.2: 20).

It is the Spirit that quickens (gives life), and as saints we do not seek the living among the dead, they are absent from the body, and now present with the Lord.

Sleep

Should the believers in Jesus Christ be taken back by the death of loved ones, and what should be the grieving process for the saints of God? Death has never been easy to deal with, it's being filled with sorrow as well as tears and emotions, so how should those who are in the body of Christ view death, and should they walk around numb and depressed, should they stop living their lives when they lose a loved one?

You and I cannot understand death, and as human beings we have all been touched by it in one way or another, some very closely as family members pass away.

I lost my wife to cancer in 1994, has this been an easy journey, if I said yes I would be lying, death is not easy especially when there are young children involved, but it is a reality, death lets us know that we have no power over life, if we did, none of us would die.

What we have learned from the word of God is that when a person who is in Christ passes away, it's not viewed the same as a person who has passed away without him as their savior.

The bible teaches the saints of God how they should deal with loss, of course in our flesh (human nature), it's difficult to apply what we are going to say here, but once we are in the Spirit (surrendered to God), **the practical application of God's word becomes clear to us.**

When a believer (also called saints, and Christians), passes away, we are to view this as a temporary sleep, when we find believers passing away it's called sleep, because it will not be for a long period of time, in fact we are told, we are absent from our bodies and present with the Lord (II Corinthians.5: 8). The saints of God are not to get caught up with sorrows like the world does, because we have the assurance from the Lord that those who have transitioned from their temporal bodies, and to a spirit body will one day be transformed and be given a glorious new body (I Corinthians.15).

Let's look at a few of those who were said to die (sleep) in Jesus. In John's record of the gospel we see Lazarus a man loved by Jesus became sick (John.11: 2) and his sisters sought Jesus to come and heal him, Jesus told his disciples that Lazarus was sleep and he (Jesus) was going to die (on the cross) so he could raise him (Lazarus) and all believers eternally.

Those around did not comprehend what Jesus meant when he said Lazarus was sleep so he then told them plainly Lazarus was dead (v.14).

Lazarus was a clear example of God's ability to raise us spiritually as well as physically from the dead.

Did Jesus love Lazarus, all indicators tells us yes he did, and yet Lazarus died, those in the flesh see death only one way, we know it only from our human perspective, but once we give ourselves over to the power of God, as Martha and Mary did, we, just like these two sisters must understand that Christ has power over even death as he would demonstrate at the grave of Lazarus.

Before we go any further I want to make a point very clear, all who pass away are seen as sleeping (*as far as their bodies are concerned*) in the grave, but there are those who have made their beds (spiritual abode) in Hell as the rich man did in the book of Luke, and those who made their beds in heaven, as we spoke of before, when we said absent from the body present with the Lord.

Sleep is a temporary rest from labor both physical and spiritual, and the bible lets us know that we will all sleep (die), and that all shall be resurrected from the dead one day also, some to everlasting life, others to everlasting judgment (Daniel.12: 2). Daniel is speaking of the two resurrections (*see chapter Two Resurrections*).

We are told that there will be a time that all who sleep (just and unjust, holy and unholy) will hear God's voice, but what follows will differ greatly depending on the individual's relationship to Christ.

Being in Christ is the key; let's look again at what the scriptures teach. Saints are told not to sorrow as those who have no hope (*in Christ*), I Thessalonians.4: 13.

This particular scripture does not suggest that believers don't feel the loss of a loved one, but the saints rest in the power of what Christ not only said but what he was able to do as well, and that was to rise from the dead (Revelations.1: 18).

We're told, because he (Christ), lives we shall live also (Romans.6: 8-11). There are those who don't believe or accept the finished work of Christ on the cross, they don't believe he was resurrected or even died for that matter, and he certainly could not be the Son of God, so the judgments of God will be on them for their unbelief (John.3: 36).

When Christ raised from the dead, he gave hope to every human being that death was not the end, and that he has power over it. Death is only a doorway that leads to eternity, either with Christ, or without him.

Here's the hope for us as believers who die (sleep) in Jesus. First, we are instructed not to sorrow as those who have no hope, as if life ceases when we pass away, for if we believe that Jesus died and rose again (*our faith in action*), even so (we also believe) those who **SLEEP IN JESUS** will God bring with him, and those who remain (at the Lord's coming) shall not go ahead of those who sleep.

The Lord himself will descend from Heaven with a shout, and with the voice of the archangel, and with the trump of God, and the dead in Christ shall rise first: and those who are alive and remain are going to be caught up (what we have called raptured) together with them in the clouds to meet the Lord in the air (this is the first part of the resurrection) and so we shall forever be with the Lord and should **COMFORT ONE ANOTHER WITH THESE WORDS** (I Thessalonians.4: 14-18).

Let's go a step further, the bible tells us that we shall not all sleep (die) before the Lord's return, in fact Paul speaking to the believers in the Corinthian church said, behold I show you a mystery, we shall not all SLEEP, but we shall all be changed, in a moment in the twinkling of an eye at the last trump, for the trumpet will sound, and the dead (sleeping) shall be raised incorruptible and we shall be changed (I Corinthians.15: 51, 52).

Deaths power will be rendered null when we have been changed, death will be swallowed up in victory (I Corinthians.15: 54).

Second, Jesus makes it very clear that he has power over death, in the book of Matthew a certain ruler came to Jesus seeking his help for his dead daughter (Matthew.9: 18). Mark lets us know the name of this man, he was Jairus, and his daughter was at the point of death and he wanted Jesus to lay hands on her that she would live (Mark.5: 22, 23), Luke lets us know this girls age was 12 (Luke.8: 42).

The scene around her was that of mourning, the music was played (Matthew.9: 23), there was weeping and much sadness (Mark.5: 38), Jesus arrived and the young girl had died, but they had no idea they were dealing with God in the flesh who had power over situations and circumstances beyond man's understanding.

Jesus said to those attending, that the girl was not dead but only sleeping (Luke.8: 52), the people laughed at this, to the point of scorning. Jesus had everyone put out of the room except Peter, James, John, and her parents. Once this was done Jesus raised the young girl from the dead presenting her back to her family (Luke.8: 54, 55).

Jesus was known for healing the sick, opening the eyes of the blind and feeding the hungry masses.

When death was spoken of, it was seen as the end of life, and once someone died, they did not come back from the grave.

Jesus called death a sleep, because everyone would be raised from the dead one day, and they would have to give an account of the things done in their bodies.

Remember the words of the Lord when he said, behold I come quickly and my reward is with me to give every man **according to his works** (Revelation.22: 12), our bodies are the temporary homes to our souls, from dust our bodies were created and to dust they will return if the Lord tarries (Ecclesiastes.12: 7).

Let's also be mindful that some sleep brings rest some torment. It's our bodies that sleep in the grave, but our souls are either in peace in paradise (Heaven) or they are tormented in Hell. Here's something to think about. When Christ spoke of the rich man and Lazarus dying, Lazarus was taken to paradise, and is seen in the bosom of Abraham while the rich man was in Hell in torment. Here's a glimpse of what happened when people died. Their bodies would sleep in the grave, but their souls would immediately be in Heaven or Hell depending on where they had placed their faith during their lifetime.

Jesus' death and resurrection freed us from the power of death, and until Jesus' death and rising from the dead, everyone who died by faith went to paradise, and not Heaven the abode of God, and there they would remain, until Jesus first rose from the dead. Jesus would be the first fruit of them that sleep.

A good example of this is seen in the book of Matthew where we are told, and the graves were opened, and many bodies of the saints which slept rose, and came out of the graves (*after Jesus' resurrection*), and went into the holy city and appeared to many (Matthew.27: 52, 53). This event took place only after Jesus was first to raise from the dead, more on this later. Jesus cannot die again, and those who are in Christ, can never die again as Christ is God's great eternal and everlasting example.

Death is made easier to understand if we see it as Christ desires us to see it, and that is, death is only a brief time of sleep for the saints of God, only to awake to a more glorious life with our Eternal Creator.

I Am the Resurrection

Jesus had a conversation with Martha, a close friend of his, concerning the death of her brother, to remind her that God is always in control of any and all situations that confronts us in our lives and that would include death. The words Jesus spoke are some of the most well-known words in scripture, many have heard them, but few understood them as we see here with Martha, Mary and the disciples as well.

I am the resurrection and the life, he that believes in me though he was dead, yet he shall live said Jesus (John.11: 25), powerful words but what do they truly mean and were they relevant?

Everything we believe as Christians rest in what Christ said here, the Apostle Paul put it this way saying, if in this life only we have hope in Christ, we are all men most miserable (I Corinthians.15: 19), and if we preach that Christ raised from the dead and he did not, then is our faith vain (I Corinthians.15: 14). Without the resurrection everything else would be a lie.

As believers our faith rest in the death, burial and resurrection of Christ known as the gospel or good news.

Resurrections are spoken of several times in scripture, and the raising of Lazarus is one of nine resurrections recorded in the bible, six in the New Testament, and three in the Old Testament.

There might be some students of the word of God who are not aware of this information, so I will cover each of them briefly.

It's important for us to understand the power of God, and why Jesus' resurrection was, and is so important to the saints of God, and the faith we preach.

(1)

Elijah and the widow's son

I Kings.17: 17-23

The first time a resurrection was performed in the bible is found in the book of Kings (I Kings.17: 17-23), where the servant of God Elijah was staying in the home of a widow woman in a loft (v.19), she was also a Gentile (none Jew), but one who believed in the one living God (v.12), her son became very sick and died (v.17), she thought it was due to some sin she had committed to bring about his death (v.18), let's be mindful of this, that being a sinner does not mean we have done anything wrong when death comes to us, or a loved one, but it is a time that we can glorify God, even in the midst of our sorrowful circumstance.

This woman was grieved, now we don't know exactly why her son died but what we can learn from it is that God had a purpose, possibly to further strengthen this Gentile woman's faith through obedience as we see after Elijah raises him from the dead and returns him to his mother (vss.20-24).

(2)

Elisha and the Shunammite woman

II Kings.4: 1- 37

The second time a resurrection is seen it's found in the book of II Kings, this time it would be by the hand of Elisha, who had seen one of the greatest miracles take place, he saw Elijah taken up to Heaven in a fiery chariot (II Kings.2: 11). Elijah did not die, and before he was taken up to Heaven, he asked Elisha what he could do for him, and Elisha's answer was that a double portion of his spirit (*faith)*, be upon him (v.9).

The second resurrection involved a Shunammite woman and her husband, they could not have children, they were kind to Elisha, even making him a place to stay in their home whenever he came through their town (4: 8-11). Elisha wanted to do something for them for all their kindness to him. Elisha told her, she and her husband would have a child, and this news shocked her so much that she asked him not to lie to her (v.16).

She conceived just as Elisha said, they had a son, and he grew and worked in the fields with his father. One day as he was working he told his father he was having pain in his head (v.19), and the father told one of the young reapers (workers), to take him to his mother, we're told he was sat on her knees until about noon, and then he died (v.20). This child was a blessing to them, a couple who could not have a child, who was blessed and now her only child was dead.

She laid his lifeless body on the bed in the man of God's room (v.21) quite possibly believing his room was a sacred place. She knew she had to do something for her child, did she know what Elisha would or might do if he came back with her? I don't believe so, but she knew he was a man of God, and that he could do something.

She travelled some miles to get to Elisha even at the risk of losing her own life (v.24) and she found him at Mt. Carmel (v.25). Elisha sent his servant ahead of them with his staff to lay on the child (v.29). The staff was a symbol of the power of God as was seen in Exodus (Exodus.2: 17; 7: 19, 20; 14: 16). God used

Aaron, Moses' brother to often perform the miracles, and in Elisha's case he sent his servant Gehazi before him, but with no affect (v.31).

Doubtlessly, there were many people who knew about the child's death, and wondered where his mother had gone, after Gehazi showed up and laid the staff upon the child's face, it was clear to everyone that he was dead. When Elisha arrived, he went into the room, and shut the door behind him. He was alone with the child and prayed (v.33), God's people don't require an audience for God to do his will or his work, those outside were wondering what Elisha would do.

He laid his body upon the body of the child, the child's flesh that was cold received warmth again (v.34), but he was not alive yet, we are told Elisha walked around the house for a few minutes, I'm sure those around wanted to know what was happening, Elisha returned to the room again placing himself on the child, the child then sneezed seven times and opened his eyes (v.35).

Elisha called Gehazi and told him to get the boy's mother, and when she came into the room he told her to take her son, her son who was dead was now alive and all who were in their company know a miracle had taken place (v.36).

(3)

Elisha's body raises dead

II Kings.13: 20, 21

This particular miracle is one of the most interesting found in the Old Testament.

It concerns the body of the prophet Elisha. There is not much said of what takes place, but it was a miracle of resurrection.

Elisha had come to the close of his ministry, and we are told he had fallen sick (*become ill*) of his sickness (II Kings.13: 14), he had given the King (Joash) instructions concerning Israel and later died (vs.15-19).

Elisha died and was buried, the exact length of time he was dead is not said, only that the Moabites invaded the land that coming year (v.20).

The Israelites were burying a man when they saw a band of men, quite possibly soldiers, since soldiers are often spoken of as bands. Those burying the man became afraid for their own lives, the funeral services had to be interrupted, they did not want to leave the body out in the open, as it might indicate someone being in the area, what follows is where we again see the marvelous working of God.

It was with haste that they cast this body into the sepulcher of Elisha, they did not know whose body was in this place they just wanted to hide the body and themselves before they could be spotted, as they let this body down into the grave it came into contact with Elisha bones and what happened next I'm sure caused them all to pause, the dead man revived and stood on his feet (v.21).

Here is a man of God who had died a little while ago whose body is laid in the grave and yet there was virtue in his body. What a beautiful picture for us to see that even our death can bring life.

Jesus said, unless a corn of wheat falls into the ground and die, it abides along, but if it dies, it brings forth much fruit (John.12: 24). The death of a saint can bring forth life.

These men possibly knew nothing of the grave, or who lay in it, they simply used it to hide a body, and then themselves. But this is a clear picture of what God has said concerning Israel by Moses, I will be gracious to whom I will be gracious and will shew mercy to whom I will shew mercy (Exodus.33: 19).

Here was an extraordinary resurrection, we know nothing about the man who was raised from the dead only that it took place. One thing is certain, it had an effect on those who witnessed it that day.

The lives of believers today should have resurrection power flowing through them to those who are spiritually dead and dying. A believer's life should be seen as a source of life in a world of darkness. There were only these three incidences of resurrections found in the Old Testament, and raising the dead was not something that only took place in the New Testament. Now let's continue by looking at those resurrections found in the New Testament by Christ and others.

(4)

The Widow's Son

Luke.7: 1-10

Jesus had just left Capernaum where he had spoken the word to bring about the healing of the son of a centurion (Luke.7: 1-10) and he went to a city called Nain, and because of the healings and other miracles that he did prior a great number of people followed him everywhere he went.

As Jesus was approaching the city there was a funeral and a dead man was being carried out, he was the only son of his mother who was a widow, she might have been well known because we are told many of the people from the city was with her (v.12).

When Jesus saw her, we are told **he had compassion on** (*for*) **her,** and told her not to weep (v.13), I'm sure his words were reassuring to her and a great comfort but he was not done, he stopped the biers (those carrying the body) and they stood still waiting to see what Jesus would do next, the words he spoke, and what occurred next amazed everyone, Jesus spoke seven words, **YOUNG MAN I SAY UNTO THEE ARISE** (v.14)

I'm sure the silence was thick as they watched to see what would take place next, the bible tells us that this young man who was dead sat up and began to speak, and Jesus delivered him to his mother (v.15).

I'm sure that the tears that flowed in sorrow, now became tears of joy. How could this be, who is this man Jesus that he even has power over death? Feeding a multitude is one thing, healing the blind and curing the sick they heard of and knew of from this man Jesus, but to raise the dead was something they had never seen anyone do.

This was one of only three resurrections performed by our Lord that is recorded in scripture. Let's take a look at the second.

(5)

Jairus' Daughter

Mark.5: 22-42

This is another of the miracles that Jesus performs by raising the daughter of Jairus, but we will speak to this in greater detail in the chapter titled "Sleep", please refer to it for the insight of this resurrection.

(6)

Lazarus

John.11: 1-47

One of the most famous, and well-known stories is that of Lazarus being raised from the dead by Jesus (John.11: 1-47). In the beginning of this chapter we referred to words spoken by our Lord to the sister of Lazarus, words that were reminders of who Christ is and what he was, and is capable of doing, words that show us that he is, was, and always will be in complete harmony with the Father.

Lazarus' death and resurrection pulled everything together, to demonstrate the authority of God the Son in life, and over death; in fact, Jesus reviews what it's like to have both a spiritual relationship, as well as an eternal relationship with God in this chapter, as he speaks to various issues of life and the afterlife.

There are a number of things to take note of, the first is, the relationship Jesus had with this family. Martha, Mary and Lazarus who were apparently close siblings, had a relationship with Christ and from all appearance Jesus would stay in their home when he visited Bethany (Matthew.21: 17), we are told when Jesus had entered into a certain village we know now to be Bethany, Martha received him into her house (Luke.10: 38), it becomes clear that Martha was the oldest of the siblings followed by Mary and the youngest would be Lazarus, Mary sat at the feet of Jesus receiving his teaching (v.39) and Martha was busy trying to serve Jesus and those who followed him, and complaining that Mary did not help her (v.40), getting the word of God was more important than having a fancy meal set (vs.41, 42). We also find that this is the same Mary that would later anoint the Lord with ointment and wipe his feet with her hair (Matthew.26: 7; Mark.14: 4).

This gives us a little insight into the characters of Martha and Mary, and from what we find in scripture this family developed and had a close relationship with the Lord. When Lazarus became ill it was very natural for these sisters to turn to Jesus, their friend, for help, as we find in John 11, their brother was sick and if anyone could help it was the Lord, but to add a sense of urgency the sisters sent word to Jesus saying the one whom he loved is sick (11: 2).

Their friendship alone should have been enough to have the Lord hurry to his sick friend. It's very easy to become complacent in our walk with the Lord, and even feel as if we are entitled to anything from the Lord we might ask of him. We should be mindful to always let it be known that if it's according to his will let it be done.

We must learn that whatever time Christ arrives is the right time even if it's at the point of death, the thief on the cross found salvation and paradise hanging from a cross and about to die (Luke.23: 39-43), whatever sins he had committed to that point, would be rendered void once he confessed Christ, and not only would he die **with Christ**, but he would die **in Christ**.

When Jesus received word of Lazarus being sick he said in effect it's no big deal, everything will be okay, his sickness is not unto death (finality), but rather for the glory of God, and that it would be used by God to also glorify Christ (John.11: 4).

John lets us know Jesus had love for Lazarus and his family (v.5), but also lets us know that this did not change Jesus' message or his ministry, and he remained where he was for 2 more days (v.6), and afterwards set his face towards Judea, and spoke about his own death, but they did not understand his words (vs.7-10).

Jesus then spoke of Lazarus again saying their friend Lazarus is sleep now, but he (Jesus) had to go so he could wake him out of his sleep (v.11), and once again they did not comprehend what Jesus was saying, so he had to make it very clear what he was saying, **LAZARUS WAS DEAD** (v.14).

How was it that Jesus knowingly let someone he cared for and love die, this same question has been asked countless times by people even today who don't understand the ways or the will of God, as Amy I spoke of earlier did not?

Let's also be mindful that the recorded history we read about took place after the events, and not during them, and were written to help us understand how God worked and continues to work. For whatsoever things were written aforetime (in the past) were written for our learning, that we through patience and comfort of the scriptures might have hope (Romans.15: 4).

The bible teaches us that **ALL THINGS WORK TOGETHER FOR GOOD to them that**

LOVE GOD, to them who are THE CALLED ACCORDING TO HIS PURPOSE (Romans.8: 28).

Although this is true, many of us have a hard time accepting it as fact, as **we look only at our pain, and not God's power.**

The death of Lazarus could also be seen as a pivotal point, there are no other resurrections in scripture performed by Christ that follows it, and it's the only one that Christ goes into detail concerning its true purpose, nature of death, and eternity.

The veil of eternity is again being drawn back to give us a glimpse into what awaits those who are in Christ once they leave here in sleep.

Martha, who represents those who worry about THINGS, heard that Jesus was finally on his way, she went out to meet him, leaving Mary with the mourners (John.11: 20), she didn't do this because she loved the Lord, she did it because she was disappointed with him, she did it to let him know he had let her family down. And had he showed up when they first sent word to him, **her brother would not have died** (v.21).

Martha was being forceful and opinionated, giving Jesus a piece of her mind, she spoke to him as if he were like an average man who had some power with God, and not as if he was indeed God in the flesh.

How easy it becomes for us to forget who Christ is because of our selfish desires.

To take away some of the disappointment in her words she said, but even now, she believed whatever Jesus asked of God he would do (v.22), as if to say even though you were late getting here you have a chance to make it up to us.

Jesus did not debate her word for word, or belittle her for what she said, he knew her flesh was also speaking as those who grieve, so instead he gave her words of assurance telling her Lazarus will rise again (v.23).

These were not satisfactory words for Martha who said she knows Lazarus will raise again in the resurrection of the last day (v.24), Martha knew what the scripture said about those who died and what becomes of them from learning the *Tanakh* (the Hebrew bible or Old Testament), but this waiting would not have been necessary if Jesus had been there sooner. **Here's a clear picture that demonstrates that knowledge of the word of God does not mean understanding it**.

Martha did not truly understand who it was that had been visiting her house and who it was that was standing before her. Martha, and Mary had Christ **visiting their home but had not invited him in their**

hearts, it's much like having a bible in our homes, reading it but never understanding its true value.

Christ shifts his conversation with Martha, he emphasizes', **I AM THE RESURRECTION** and the life and that anyone who believes in him even though he were dead (physically) they shall never die (eternally), and those who live, and believe in Christ, would never die (eternally), he asked Martha did she believe (and accept) this (vs.25, 26)?

Now the door of salvation for Martha swings open with her declaring, *Yes Lord, I believe you are the Christ the Son of God who should come into the world* (v.27).

Martha's attitude had to change about herself, and her relationship to God, which would be more important than what was going to follow in her life concerning her brother.

Martha had experienced a resurrection in her spirit, she understood now just who Jesus really is, and was ready to share it with her sister Mary, who she called secretly (privately), and told her that Jesus wanted to see her (v.28). **There's excitement in salvation.**

There's a spiritual understanding that accompanies our accepting who Christ is, and it gives new insight to the passionate commitment we have about him, and our service to him, Martha was born again.

Now, Mary had to see Jesus, (*bear in mind that they had the written word of God but had no real understanding of the living word of God, or in more simple terms they did not know how to spiritually apply God's word, a problem shared with so many of us today*).

Funerals are usually the ultimate time of sadness, as it reminds each of us that we do not live in these bodies forever, and that one day we must leave them behind.

There were many people gathered together with Mary at her home, who also followed her as she left the house thinking she was going to the grave site to mourn her brother there (v.31).

Mary's complaint appears to be the same as her older sister, that had the Lord been there sooner her brother would not have died (v.32), but you will notice there was a difference in how Mary approached Jesus, she fell down at his feet (a show of humility) something Martha did not do.

Although their words were similar, the attitude behind them was immensely different, Mary humbled herself before Christ, with Martha we find no tears, but here with Mary she is weeping (v.33), and we find

Jesus groaned in his spirit (v.34) and did something we had not heard of before in the scriptures, **Jesus wept** (v.35).

There are many opinions and views concerning why Jesus wept, some have said it was because he was moved deeply because he saw how much sorrow that sickness and death brought to the lives of people, others have said he wept because they did not understand the power of God and looked at things purely from the physical perspective. Later we find in scripture as Christ was being led to his death and falling under the weight of the cross, women were seen weeping for him, Jesus told them not to weep for him but rather for themselves and their children (Luke.23: 26-28).

Christ was in a human body and therefore was also moved as would any human being when it pertains to death.

There are at least two views when it comes to death, there is a secular view, and the spiritual view. The secular view of death is that of finality, that there is nothing that follows death; it is the end of existence, and there is no after life, no heaven or hell, the teaching is, eat drink and be merry for tomorrow we die, the attitude is one of, do whatever you want, it doesn't matter when you die it's all forgotten.

A world without Christ is one built around sin and sinning, and lack of morals. It's no wonder so many weep with such sadness at the death of a loved one, as they live their lives without hope.

The religious (*not necessarily Christian or truly spiritual*) believes that there is life after death, that there is another life, a richer and more beautiful one than the one they are leaving behind. A life that has God's love as it's center and Christ as Savior, it's a life lived with the hope of being resurrected, given a new body, and having everlasting life, This was the resurrection that Martha was referring to for her brother and all believers.

Of all the miracles that Jesus performed, raising the dead would be the most important of all of them, and the reason will become clearer in a few moments.

Jesus went to the grave of his friend Lazarus and told them to remove the stone sealing the entrance. Martha became concerned saying that Lazarus had been dead four days and his body would be decaying and would be beginning to stink at that point (John.11: 39).

Jesus gently reminds Martha of the words he had already confirmed with her (v.40), all she needed to do is exercise her faith.

Many of us today miss out on what the Lord can do in our lives because we are too busy questioning, doubting and not believing or walking by our faith.

Once the stone was removed, Jesus looked Heavenward and gave a simple prayer of thanks being already assured what his Father wanted, Jesus prayed aloud to the extent he wanted those who were listening to know he was connected to God in Heaven and that God had sent him (v.42).

What follows is the foundation of faith for all those who are in Christ, Jesus looking towards the tomb cried out with a loud voice, with power, and with authority and said Lazarus come forth (v.43).

God the Son in the person of Jesus Christ called out to one of his own, one he had a personal relationship with to come forth. Jesus was very specific and called Lazarus by name, not long before this event Jesus taught his disciples that he was the shepherd of the sheep, and his sheep know his voice and would not follow another (John.10: 4, 5).

There's a remarkable consistency to the words and actions of Jesus as they are compared, his words spoke of his mission and his actions defined it. Jesus said he was the resurrection and the life and now at the tomb of Lazarus he was about to demonstrate this as fact. Jesus called out to one of his sheep Lazarus, no one went into the tomb to bring him out, we are told that he that was dead came forth, Lazarus was still bound hand and foot in his grave clothes, and Jesus instructed those around to free him from his death clothes (v.43). This third resurrection by Christ is the last one he performs personally, but there are yet a few more I would also mention.

Special Note

As we have seen Christ is indeed the resurrection and life, everyone who was raised from the dead would die again according to the flesh, so in order to live forever someone would have to lead the way, to be the example, someone would have to die and be raised again that would never die again as proof there is everlasting life.

Jesus said he would lay down his life and that he had the power to take it up again, this power comes from his Father (John.10: 17, 18).

There are a couple of things we must know about Jesus' resurrection, the first being this, **NO ONE who died** went to Heaven before Christ resurrection. Jesus would be the first, (*first fruit*) of those who slept, to raise from the dead forever (I Corinthians.12: 20 compare also Leviticus.23: 9-14).

In the book of Matthew, we find the graves of **many of THE SAINTS** that died were opened and they came out of their graves after Jesus' resurrection and walked around the holy city (Matthew.27: 52, 53).

We also know our bodies life is in our blood (Leviticus.17: 11-14) our bodies are dependent on blood, and that without it we could not live, Jesus lost much blood on the cross, it was also a contributing factor in his death, Jesus was our blood offering to God, the atonement for sin, and our physical existence depends on the blood coursing through our veins.

Those who were raised from the dead in scripture had one thing in common; they still had blood in their bodies, even today those who claim they died and came back from the dead remained warm, they maintained blood in them for this miracle of being resurrected back to life.

I would like for you to consider what happened to Jesus when he died. First, He did not receive a transfusion to replenish the blood he had lost.

Second, we believe he actually died on the cross, as was indicated by his being pierced in his side by a soldier (John.19: 32-34).

Third, He was buried, and guards were posted at his tomb to ensure that his disciples did not come and remove his body, and say he rose from the dead

(Matthew.27: 62-66). There was no way humanly possible for anyone to steal Jesus' body, these were Roman guards who were accustomed to long nights without sleep and would defend their post to the death if need be.

All four of the gospels agree that Jesus did rise from the grave (Matthew.28: 1-10; Mark.16: 1-14; Luke.24: 1-35; John.20: 1-14).

Remarkably as John concludes is writing he lets his readers know there were many things Jesus did that were not recorded in the gospel (John.21: 25).

Was Jesus' resurrection real, if not, many people went to their graves defending and dying for a lie, the Apostle Paul concerning the reality of the resurrection writes, Moreover, brethren, I declare unto you the gospel which I preached unto you, which also ye have received, and wherein ye stand;

By which also ye are saved, if ye keep in memory what I preached unto you, unless ye have believed in vain.

For I delivered unto you first of all that which I also received, how that Christ died for our sins according to the scriptures;

And that he was buried and that he rose again the third day according to the scriptures:

And that he was seen of Cephas, then of the twelve:

After that, he was seen of above five hundred brethren at once; of whom the greater part remain unto this present, but some are fallen asleep.

After that, he was seen of James; then of all the apostles.

And last of all he was seen of me also, as of one born out of due time (I Corinthians.15: 1-8).

Jesus' resurrection turned a new page concerning eternity; he bridged the gap from the Old Testament (covenant) to the New Testament (covenant agreement), Christ brought clarity to God's word.

Jesus raising others from the dead would mean nothing if he did not do so himself, and how can someone who has been dead for thousands of years come back to life? When we as human beings think on the natural plane it's impossible to grasp spiritual things as this, but on the supernatural level and by faith this becomes clear, read what Paul had to say in I Corinthians.15: 35-50 about the resurrection bodies.

(7)

Peter Raises Tabitha

Acts.9: 36-42

Before Jesus ascended back to the Father, he had told his disciples that the works he did, they would also do, these would be signs (physical proofs) that Christ was with the disciples (later called Apostles).

While Peter was in a village called Lydda a city not far from Joppa we learn of a young godly woman who was also a disciple named Tabitha (which also means Dorcas or gazelle), she was a woman who was full of good works (Act.9: 36).

Tabitha was sick, how long she was sick is not known or what the sickness was but she died, and when she was washed (*prepared for burial*) her body was laid in an upper chamber (v.37). Word got to them that Peter was not far away they sent for him to come and not delay (v.38). Their expectation was that Peter could do something if he got there soon enough. This was very much like what took place with Martha and Mary concerning Lazarus and Jesus.

Peter had healed a crippled man who had been that way for eight years in a neighboring town (Acts.9: 32-35) and word spread quickly and those at Joppa must have heard about this miracle and sent for Peter.

When Peter arrived, he was met by mourners before he could go in to see her, and friends of Tabitha who loved her showed Peter the things Tabitha had done for them, her works spoke for her.

There was weeping because they had lost a godly friend in Tabitha. Peter put everyone out, kneeled down and prayed, then turning towards her body spoke only two words, TABITHA ARISE. She opened her eyes, and when she saw Peter she sat up (v.40). Peter then took her by the hand and lifts her (helps her to her feet), he then called the saints and the widows and presented her alive to them (v.41).

This miracle was known throughout all Joppa and just like those in Lydda, many believed in the Lord because of it (v.42).

(8)

Paul is Raised From the Dead

Acts.14: 19, 20; II Corithians.12: 1-5

One of the most interesting resurrections might be this eighth one, that involved Paul the Apostle, there are those who have varying opinions about what took place, I will share what I have found in scripture and you can form your own view.

Paul and Barnabas were in Iconium sharing the word of God concerning Christ and salvation with the Jews and Gentiles, and many believed on both sides, but conflict arose by unbelieving Jews who felt threatened by this word of Faith, speaking evil against those who believed (Acts.14: 2).

The city was divided because of their teaching, some believed in the Greek gods (Gentiles) and others the Jewish God the Apostles spoke of (v.4).

Some of the people felt they were better off before Paul and Barnabas showed up and sought to stone them, Paul and Barnabas were aware of this and left and preached in the cities around it (vs.5-7).

The people saw them as nothing more than mere men, that was until Paul performed a miracle on a man at Lystra who could not walk from his mother's womb (v.8), as the man listened to Paul speak, he stared at Paul, listened intently, and Paul saw his faith (v.9) and told him in a loud voice to stand on his feet and **the man responded immediately** (v.10).

When the people saw this miracle they spoke in their language (Lycao'nia) saying, "The gods have come down to us in the likeness of men" (v.11), calling Barnabas Jupiter (Zeus) and Paul Mercurious (Hermes) since Paul was the chief speaker of the two (v.12).

They tried to make a sacrifice to them, and they (Paul and Barnabas) rent (tore) their clothes telling them they were not gods they were only men and men should not be worshiped as God (vs.13-15).

There were some Jews who had followed them from Antioch and Ico'nium who persuaded the people that Paul should be stoned (v.19), the reason is not given but possibly for their believing he was pretending to be a god, or defaming theirs.

Paul was stoned by the people, and they took his body outside the city and dumped it leaving him for dead. Now the bible does not say specifically that Paul died, but if you read II Corinthians chapter 12: 1-5 we find that Paul is taken up into the third Heaven and sees some remarkable things, could this have taken place when he was stoned and left for dead, or dead, outside the city? It's very possible, in this resurrection we find the disciples stood around his body and Paul rose up (Acts.14: 20).

The Lord was not done with Paul yet, there was still much he had to do as we see in that verse where he and Barnabas went into the city and the following day went to Derbe.

(9)

Eutychus

Acts. 20:7-12

The ninth resurrection spoken of here, was performed by Paul while he was in Asia Minor. It was the days of unleavened bread, and on the first day of the week (*the time of gathering for believers since it was on the first day of the week that Jesus raised from the dead*), what we call Sunday today.

Paul shared the word of God with those who had gathered with him to break bread and remember the Lord and all he had done for them. Paul knew he would be leaving the next day, so he shared the word of God with them all evening until midnight (Acts.20: 7).

We're told there were many lights in that upper room that night, in other words there were many people there (v.8)

There was a young man Eutychus, sitting in the window (*propping himself on the window ledge*), fell into a deep sleep, he had a willing spirit to be there and to hear what was being said by Paul, but his flesh was weak (*tired*), much in the way as Peter, James, and John's was in the garden with Christ (Matthew.26: 41).

Eutychus fell asleep but was in the wrong place to do so and falls from the window, not inside the room but backwards from the third loft and died (Acts.20: 9).

What a horrible thing to happen, Paul was preaching, and those in attendance were remembering all the Lord had done, and Paul shared with them how the Lord was working in his life, then suddenly there's a scream, a young man had fallen from the window to his death. What did this child do wrong, and why did he have to die like that?

Paul's message was interrupted but not his ministry, the preaching stopped but the power remained. I'm sure most every eye was now on Paul, what was he going to do? Paul goes down and assessed things, he fell on him and embraced his body with his (*much like we read with Elijah, and Elisha in the Old Testament*), and Paul reassured them and let everyone know it was okay, not to worry themselves, the young man's life was still in him (v.10), in effect what Paul was saying was this, the young man is now only sleeping. Paul went back to sharing with them until the morning and then left (v.11) and we find the young man alive and the family was comforted both physically as well as spiritually (v.12).

The resurrection of the dead is vital and very important to the Christian doctrine; this is why this is the longest chapter in this book. I want each of you to have a clear understanding of what the resurrection means to the saints of God.

There are a number of resurrections, two in fact, and we will be looking at who will take part in them, and which one. There is no general, or one massive resurrection as some have taught and believed (*more on that in my book "And the books were opened"*).

Two Resurrections

It must be also said that there are two resurrections or better, two parts to the resurrection, and although we would like to believe everyone will go to heaven, this is not the case, and it must likewise be said that some of our loved ones when they pass from this life, will go to a place of torment, followed by everlasting punishment.

Growing up, and young in the faith I'd been taught like many others, that there was only one resurrection, a general resurrection of the last day; it's been taught by preachers and churches and embraced by many more.

I've come to learn biblically, that there are two very distinct aspects of the resurrections spoken of in scripture, that some evangelicals have ignored. The reason for this is not clear to me, perhaps it's because they don't want to hurt anyone's feelings when it comes to their loved ones passing away, or they may not clearly understand it themselves. But the fact is, everyone will take part in either the first of the second resurrection, but not both. Blessed are they that have their part in the first resurrection (Revelation.20: 6).

The rich man in Luke's record of the gospel who found himself in Hell, was not concerned with how he got there, he knew full well what he had done in life. The rich man's concern would turn to his brothers, not even how they would feel. His fear was that they would end up where he was, and that they needed to know about that place (Hell), and not end up there as he did (Luke.16: 27, 28).

The bible speaks of resurrections, there will be at least two of them, first **1**) the resurrection of life and second **2**) the resurrection to death or judgment, they are not the same nor will they take place at the same time.

Resurrection means something has died and was brought back, but resurrection does not mean that what has been brought back will continue to have life.

Daniel speaking said, many of them that sleep in the dust of the earth shall awake, some to everlasting life (*first aspect of the resurrection for the righteous*) and some to everlasting contempt (*the wicked judged and cast into the lake of fire*), examine Daniel.12: 2 and compare Revelation.20: 5.

The bible teaches us that, Hell was prepared for Satan and his angels (Matthew.25: 41). Man was created for joy, by God, to live happy in paradise and live forever with the Lord.

The first part of the first resurrection will include all the Old Testament Saints, all the New

Testament (Church) Saints, and all the tribulation Saints. This resurrection is for believers only.

The second part of the resurrection is for those who rejected God, faith, and his Son. The rich man who is in hell will remain there until after the thousand-year reign of Christ, and then he will be cast alive, body and soul into Gehenna (the Lake of fire).

Christ gave this parable of this rich man as an example of what will take place for all those who reject the Son of God. Let's not fool ourselves; all our loved ones will not be getting into heaven. Jesus said only those who do the will of his Father will enter in (Matthew.7: 21).

In order to enter into the House of God we must have the Key, and Jesus said he has the keys to Hell and death (Revelation.1: 18).

It's unimaginable for any of us to think that one of our loved ones might end up in a place of torment and eternal separation from God. Maybe hell does not exist and is only a place made up by man to scare people into submission to a God, who also does not exist.

Let's go with that for a moment, the "what if" scenario. What if Hell does not exist, then it stands to reason that Heaven would not exist also, that it is no more than a made-up place from the imagination of man to control the weak, and simple-minded people through fear.

For a minute consider the following, we know there are good and bad people that are on earth, they cannot be treated the same as they have taken different paths in life, "what if" some individuals have taken the path of evil, they're violence, destructive and murderers, and this is what fills their thoughts continuously. Now "what if" on the other hand you have those who obey the law, help others, are not violent, and demonstrate no evil intent. Should killers and murderers be allowed to roam free and be allowed among those having exhibited none of these same attributes?

Man in his wisdom thought it wise to separate the good from evil, maybe it was just a whim of course, and accidental thought, a fleeting assumption, that good and evil should not reside together and the solution was to build a place for those who are evil to be housed for their evil deeds, man's answer was **JAILS and PRISONS**.

If man thought it wise to separate good from evil why should we think any less of God, who is creator of all things. Laws govern how we should live our lives among one another, and they are based on the things of Heaven.

Evil is not allowed to remain among the good; it is purged and set aside to be dealt with at a later time, possibly through the court system, again a pattern after things of Heaven. Instead of a Jail there is Hell, like Jail it's a place that lacks freedom, mobility and comfort (*well not completely, now prisoners have all the comforts of living as if not in a prison at all, prisons are now more like resorts*).

The evil that man has done, is on the Lord's docket and will be brought into God's court of justice and judgment with every hidden or secret thing (Ecclesiastes.12: 14).

Those who are in this "Jail Hell" will remain there until **THE GREAT WHITE THRONE** judgment where all accounts will be known and judgment rendered as the books will be opened and their works, words, and witness will be known and the verdict read, and those who are in this second resurrection will be cast alive into the lake of fire (Revelation20: 11-15).

The second resurrection (of damnation) is not for those who are believers but rather those who are not believers and who rejected the ministry of the Lord Jesus Christ. Will there be some of our loved ones there, undoubtedly. The saints will judge the world (I Corinthians.6: 2) and we shall be like Christ (I John.3: 2) as the wicked stand before us they will see loved ones who have made it into Heaven, but here's what will be sad, that loved one will not know them in return, but hear, the word of Christ when he said, "I never knew you depart from me" (Matthew.7: 23).

The rich man in Hell recognized Lazarus, but Lazarus is not said to have acknowledged the rich man. The rich man had one major concern and that was for his family members, he did not want them to end up in the place he did.

The "what if" scenario would be great if there was no evil, and no murders and everyone was good (godly). However, this is not the case. When the bible says all have sinned and come short of the glory of God (Romans.3: 23) and the wages of sin is death (Romans.6: 23), it becomes clear that all of us were working for sins wages.

In Christ, when we look upon sin we will see only sinful people who have rejected salvation in the Lord's Christ, we will not see them as friends, or even family members, and we will have the nature as well as the mind of Christ (Philippians.2: 5).

Many will stand before God in this second part of the resurrection but not a word will be spoken from the accused, the books will be opened, and everyone will be judged from what has been written therein. The books will have, 1) their words, 2) their works, and 3) their witness. Hell is just the stop over until the lake of fire.

The rich man pleaded and said to Abraham; send Lazarus back to his home and to his brothers to let them know about that place (Hell), surely, they will believe if someone was to come back from the dead. Abraham said they have Moses and the prophets (*the word of God, the Bible*), if they do not believe it what good would it do if someone were to raise from the dead (Luke.16:28-31).

We put little time in considering where we will spend eternity. Or where our loved ones go once, they transition from this life.

Changed

Death divides and separates even if only temporarily from our love ones, death is life's enemy and it will be the last enemy to be destroyed according to scripture (I Corinthians.15: 26). We're told the corruptible (*decaying flesh*) must put on incorruption (*spirituality*), and the mortal shall put on immortality. Then shall be brought to pass the saying that was written, Death is swallowed up in victory, O death where is your sting, O grave where is your victory?

The sting of death is sin and sin's strength was the law (I Corinthians.15: 53-57).

Jesus, is said to have the keys to Hell and death, so we have no more to fear in either of them because our lives are hidden in Christ in God (Colossians.3: 3), as Christ has overcome the world so have we.

Christ put on a glorified body after his resurrection, and this made it somewhat difficult to recognize him as the two on the Emmaus road demonstrated when Christ walked with them, and they did not know it was him until the breaking of bread (Luke.24: 13-32).

As the two from Emmaus were sharing with the disciples that the Lord had appeared to them, Christ, suddenly stood in the midst of them, it so frightened them that they thought they had seen a spirit (*ghost*), and Jesus had to calm them down. We see they did not know it was him until he showed them the wounds in his hands and feet, even telling them to touch him, and handle him saying, **a spirit has not flesh and bones Jesus tells them**, as he did (Luke.24: 36-39).

Mary Magdalene was outside the empty tomb weeping when Jesus drew near to her and asked why she was crying, she thought he was the gardener, and thought this gardener might have taken Jesus' body away. She did not see his true form until he called her by name, it was then, her eyes were opened, and she recognized him (John.20: 13-16).

The disciples had gone back to fishing, and caught nothing that night, the next day Jesus stood on the shore, but the disciples again didn't know it was him (John.21: 3-7).

Just as Christ has a glorified body every believer will also receive one as well. Our bodies will be changed, in a moment, in the blink of an eye (I Corinthians.15: 52).

Some have questioned this statement saying how this can be, with man it would be impossible (*to make spiritual change*), but with God all things are possible (Matthew.19: 26).

When Stephen, a man of God was faced with his own mortality, and pending death, being placed in a pit about to be stoned to death for his testimony, showed no fear for the witness he had in Christ, Stephen gave one of the greatest sermons of his life (Acts.6: 8-7: 60).

Stephen fell asleep the scriptures tell us under the stoning, but remarkably we hear him say the heavens opened and he saw the Son of man (Jesus) standing on the right hand of God (Acts.7: 56). Whatever pain you and I would associate with stoning, it was not there, but Jesus was, and not only comforted Stephen, but welcomed him into glory.

It's my belief that God's loving arms of protection surrounds us as believers when we make the transition from this life to the afterlife.

Stephen did not cry out for his accusers to stop, he instead asked that their sin not be held against them (v.60). What purpose does death have, and what is its role? Death changes the lives of the living.

Death clearly shows us how short our lives truly are in this world, a vapor that is seen today and gone tomorrow (James.4: 14) and the role of death is to have us to move closer to our Lord and savior, and not live in fear of it as it looms closer to us, part of the mystery of death is not knowing when it will arrive.

Stephens death was to the glory of God, and it would ultimately help lead to the conversion of Saul (Acts.22: 1-20). Stephen was a **man of faith** and **full of the Holy Ghost** (Acts.6: 5), these are two main components to the Christian faith, our faith is what gives us victory over the world (I John.5: 4), and the Holy Spirit guides us, teaches us, and opens God's word to us (John.16:13-15).

Before we can have this eternal transformation spoken of, we must go through a spiritual one first. Here's what the word of God tells us. If anyone is in Christ they become (*or better are becoming*) a new creature (*creation*), old things are passed (*passing*) away, behold all things are new (II Corinthians.5: 17), and we are to be transformed by the renewing (*changing attitude*) of our minds, that we can prove what is God's good, acceptable and perfect will (Romans.12: 2).

Spiritual change has physical effects, when we have the mind of Christ we cannot remain as we were, we begin to act as Christ acted and we will even begin to look different from the world in how we speak, remembering this, if any one speaks let them speak as the Oracle of God (I Peter.4: 11), and God's word should dwell in the saints richly (Colossians.3: 16).

When we declare Christ as our Lord and Savior we have died to self, look at how the Apostle Paul put it, *I am crucified with Christ nevertheless I live; yet not I, but Christ lives in me: and the life I now live in the flesh I live by the faith of the Son of God, who loved me and gave himself for me* (Galatians.2: 20).

We must see ourselves as dying to our flesh spiritually which opens the door for us to receive our new glorified bodies once we have been resurrected.

In order to live forever we must be willing to crucify our fleshly desires, our sinful urges and bury them in spirit, and live our new lives for the glory of God in Christ Jesus. Death to the flesh brings life in the Spirit, and if we walk in the Spirit we will not fulfill the lust (*cravings*) of the flesh (Galatians.5: 16).

Paul said because of his faith, he died daily (I Corinthians.15: 31), he was constantly under attack for his faith and belief in Jesus, particularly on the matter of Jesus' resurrection from the dead (Acts.17: 16-32; 23: 6-8; 24: 14-21;), if the resurrection is real and true then everything Jesus said pertaining to it would also be true, and this would be bad for all other religious organizations that downplay Christ and his ministry.

Every believer's hope rests in the power of the resurrection, it is the ultimate change awaiting all saints of God at the Lords coming. We have been given a new Spirit and we await the new bodies yet to come.

What kind of bodies will those raised from the dead have (I Corinthians.15: 35)? It will be like Christ, and just as he was tangible so also will those he raise, but with one major difference, there will be no need of blood in their bodies, remember what we said in the opening of this chapter, a spirit does not have flesh and bone.

Now pay close attention to what Paul says here, **flesh and blood cannot inherit the kingdom of God** (I Corinthians.15: 50). It is the Spirit that quickens (*gives life*) John.6: 63.

The length of time an individual is dead means nothing to God, and where the body is located is also known to God, (Revelations.20: 13). David asked a rhetorical question once saying, where could he go to hide from God's Spirit or hide from his presence, he said if he ascended up to heaven the Lord would be there, and if he made his bed in Hell the Lord would see him even there (Psalms.139: 7, 8).

Death brings change, emotional, physical and most of all spiritual change, it affects every human being in some way, and every living creature. How we react or respond to death will depend on what we think we know about it, what we believe, understand, and are willing to accept about it.

No More Tears

Jesus said, in this world you shall have tribulations (John.16: 33). In the book of Job, it's said, man born of a woman is of a few days, and full of trouble (Job.14: 1).

Every child born into this world brings the parents both joy and sorrow, there is the happiness of having a new life to cherish and love, but also a sadness of not knowing what will become of that child as they reach maturity. Will they love the Lord or reject him? Will they develop a ministry for the Lord or become a murderer? Will the child become rooted in God's word or followers of the world?

Having children does not mean they will follow in the steps of their parents, (*sometimes that's a good thing as there are some parents going down a dark path*).

As parents we are admonished to train up our children in the way they should go that when they are old, they will not depart from them (Proverbs.22: 6). Sometimes, this is done with many tears being shed. Given time to grow, every human being will choose and decide on the path they want to follow for themselves, good or evil.

Death has no age restrictions or color divides, death is not limited to any one culture more than another, **WE ALL DIE**, as to how and when this will take place is the great mystery before us.

Let's look at a man who loved the Lord, prayed regularly, and made offerings for not only himself, but even for his children who were adults and not in the home. He was upright, and shunned evil (Job.1: 1). He had seven sons and three daughters (v.2).

The man was named Job; he was wealthy, in fact he was the wealthiest man in the east (v.3), Job was a praying man, he not only loved the Lord, but he loved his children also, and even though they were adults he made offering to the Lord for them just in case some of them sinned unknowingly (v.5).

What follows is a good example of the rain falling on the just, those who it appears have done nothing wrong but evil befalls them. Here in the book of Job we see a clear picture of good and evil at work, how there is spiritual wickedness in high places and even who, and what, is behind the evil that comes in our lives.

The godly are not exempt from evil, in fact the godly are attacked for the purpose of destroying their faith, and if not their faith, their testimony, and for them to give in to their flesh, to resist God (*his Word,*

Spirit) and turn to cursing God rather than serving him (Job.1: 6-11).

Satan wanted to TEST JOB, to prove Job was wasting his time serving God, and that God did not care for him or about him or his family.

Jesus called Satan, the TEMPTER (tester, instigator, troublemaker, agitator, and deceiver) Matthew.4: 3; Luke.4: 2.

Note that Job's attack gives us a look behind the spiritual curtain to see what takes place in each of our lives as it pertains to good as well as evil. Many if not all of us know evil exist, we're just not willing to confront it or willing to admit it's real. Evil does not just happen no more than good just happens.

There's not a single individual among us who has not been tempted by the evil one to do evil (rebel, sin). Satan has the same desire as God, he wants to be worshiped (Luke.4: 4-8). Satan said he would **"be like the most High"** (Isaiah.14: 14), and if that means destroying every human being in the process to accomplish this goal, Satan is more than willing to do so. **It's a spiritual power struggle for supremacy**.

Now, it must be said that TEMPTATION IS NOT SIN but can lead to sin, and each of us is tempted to do evil in the hope that it will produce sin (*rebellion*) in our lives by the actions that follow. Satan hopes it would be in defiance of God, and to show him that we are the gods of our own lives not Him. What was Job's temptation (test), it was to blame God for all his losses.

Job received four messengers to let him know what had taken place with his possessions as well as his children (Job.1: 13- 19).

As human beings we are moved to set blame to someone and in most cases it's God. We know Job was a righteous man, and was aware of the power of God, and how sacrifices should be made for sin.

Job was a good example of what the Lord has for us, especially those of us who walk and live by our faith.

Job in the face of most profound tragedies, one most of us can only imagine taking place, he did not react emotionally but responded spiritually to it.

Instead of pointing his finger or wagging his fist to heaven, he got up, rent his clothes (*a show of anguish and sorrow*), shaved his head and fell down on the ground (*usually face down*) and did what many of us don't do when faced with so great a pain, HE WORSHIPPED (v.20).

Job had just lost all of his children and most of his possessions but instead of reacting on what we call the human level he moved immediately to the spiritual level.

Job did not assume that anything he had, belonged to him, that he had worked hard for it, and that he earned what he had as the thinking is today. Job did not think in that way because he understood the nature of God, he knew the word of God, and felt the power of God. So, Job went immediately into the presence of God by worship.

What was Job's response to all that had taken place, he said he came into this world naked from his mother's womb (v.21), and it was the Lord that gave him all that he had in his possession, and it was in the power of the Lord to remove it from him also (v.22).

Instead of blaming the Lord, Job blessed the Lord, and in all that he endured we are told that Job did not sin in this matter or charge (*blame*) God foolishly (v.23).

What makes Job so different; after all he lost not one child but all ten children, Job did not have a pity party nor was he consumed by guilt or look for a reason to turn away from God. **When the storm raged in Job's life, he ran to God, and not away from him?**

What is it that made Job turn to God and not away from him? Well, I believe in part, it has to do with distractions. In this modern time we live in, we have allowed countless things to come between us and the Lord?

Television, radio, books. Cell phones and movies all influence our lives today; families are distant from one another because of these common temptations.

We can see these things as tools that can benefit and aid us in our commitment and walk with the Lord, but they are often used to cause doubt and confusion in our lives, and bringing our lust for things, to the forefront in our lives.

Think about it for a moment, as you grew up what influenced you the most, what dominated the majority of your thoughts and time, was it the bible, the church, or Jesus Christ?

What many of us think we know about Christ or the bible comes from what we are told in the Christmas story of the baby born in Bethlehem.

Our conscience is bombarded with so many views and beliefs that it becomes difficult at times to decide what to do, but not impossible. What it takes is focus, we have to manage what we allow to have room in our thoughts, it will always come down to the things we give the most thoughts that will have the greatest influence in our lives.

External influences have a great impact on us, but it's the individual internal decision-making process that ultimately leads us it's called choice.

What do we mean by this, simply this, it's not what others say or do, this is not what makes us do the things we do, it's our personal belief system that we build our lives around that does.

Influence is brought into reality by individual temptation and its personal application after careful consideration of fleshly fulfillment that motivates actions.

Sounds confusing, it's not, I'll put it another way, WE choose to do what WE want to do.

With everything that took place in Job's life we don't hear him cursing God, and yet he could have chosen to do so, after all it's only human to do so. But his wife on the other hand had something to say, her thought process was not the same as her husband.

Her children were all dead. The babies she gave birth to are no longer among the living; their homes were destroyed, and land taken. We don't know Job's wife by name, but she was certainly a grieving mother and the pain must have become unbearable for her.

I'm sure her weeping was heard throughout the land as word traveled round about, she might have become depressed, mad and even angry, and she probably cried until she could cry no more. Tears turned to anger and frustration with God.

We can only imagine her anguish, she had ten funerals for her loved ones, and she like Job would have to decide what to do with all the pain she was faced with. What actions would accompany her loss?

It's always easy to say what we'll do when we are not caught in the storms of life. Certainly, we would like to believe we would do the right thing, but this is not often the case, and it's clearly evident if we are walking in the flesh, or in the Spirit by the actions that follow.

As we continue to navigate our way through the scriptures it's important for us to know why we have the Bible in the first place, and why it was written.

All scriptures are given by the inspiration of God, (*God given, appointed*), and is profitable for doctrine (*teaching*), for reproof, for correction, for instruction in righteousness (II Timothy.3: 16).

The bible was not written for our own private interpretation, the prophecy did not come by the will (*thoughts*) of man, but holy men spoke as they were moved (*prompted, guided*) by the Holy Spirit (II Peter.1: 20, 21), we are further told that the things written aforetime (in times past) were written for our learning, that we through PATIENCE and COMFORT of the scriptures might (should) have HOPE (Romans.15: 4), and that we should compare spiritual things to spiritual (I Corinthians.2: 13).

Life is filled with continuity, how one thing ties into another; it's a clear picture of how all life no matter how distant they seem are universally connected.

Job lost his family, and even his health was attacked, and those who sit on the sidelines often see things only the way they want to see them, not the way they are.

Job's life and lifestyle was under attack; his faith was put under fire. Job's life is AN EXAMPLE of how we should face life's uncertainties, from losing our health, to losing loved ones.

Instead of looking up and shaking our fist towards Heaven, we should be lifting up clasped hands and praying to the Lord that he would give us clarity and understanding of his will, in the situations we find ourselves in.

Our life expectancy in this world is short, 70, 80, 100 years, or a little more, the bible tells us that a thousand years to the Lord, is but a yesterday if we compare our lives to the Lord (Psalms.90: 4).

The day is coming when there will be no more tears, no more pain and suffering, and death will be no more.

In the book of Ecclesiastes, we find there is a time to be born, and a time to die (Ecclesiastes.3: 2).

There is a time to weep, and a time to laugh, a time to mourn and a time to dance (Ecclesiastes.3: 4).

The unfortunate side of life is, that death is a part of it, since Adam's sin in the garden. Physical death was passed on to every living thing. Our restoration began with God sending his only Son to die for our sin (John.3: 16-18), and it is faith we must now have in Christ finished work on the cross.

Jesus' death and resurrection by faith is the reason believers now have hope, and we have passed from death to life.

Don't misunderstand what I am saying. I am not saying that we should not sorrow, feel sadness, or feel grief when loved ones pass from this life, that would be almost inhuman, but, what I am passing along is this, that our grief should not be like the worlds grief, and our sorrow is not in the same way as those who don't live their lives in the comfort of God's eternal promises.

In My Heart

I was asked why a book about death and what made me an authority on it. Unquestionably I am not an authority in this area, but I have had experiences with death over the years as others.

I'm sure there are many whose life, if a side by side comparison was made, mine would not compare with there's when it comes to suffering. My goal here is only to let you, as the reader know that I can identify with various aspects of death on a personal level.

Personal experience gives an individual the right to speak on specific levels and topics. It does not make one an expert, but it does show an awareness with minimum knowledge of the topic at hand, as they mature emotionally, but more importantly mature spiritually.

Our understanding of life and death changes constantly. As a child I had no concept of death, or life for that matter, I knew babies were being born and that people were dying but it had no real impact on me apart from my feeling sad because the adults were sad, and crying around me, all of this becomes different when there's a personal connection to the loss.

Timothy White, Sr.

A child's question is often "where do people go when they die"? The answer is usually, "they go to heaven", but then I often wondered, **if Heaven is nice and is the place where everyone wants to go, why were so many people crying and screaming when a loved one has gone there**? As a child no one could explain Heaven, only express their hurt and pain when someone died.

As a child I thought as a child, seeing death as a sleep, and that everyone would wake up soon, but over the years I learned this was not completely true, and that good people are not the only ones who die, everyone dies, young and old alike.

As a young man the first closeup understanding of death came when my sister Ava passed away, and although this took place in the late1960's it remains a part of my memories even to this day. **When someone passes away does not mean they go away**, and it does not mean we forget them, in fact they live every time we think of them.

Some memories are powerfully positive; some can be negative, if we know loved ones have not been treated well while they lived. My sister Ava was a bright light that God had shined in our house for 11years, unfortunately sometimes we are too busy doing what we want to do to see these lights, and it becomes clear only when that light is taken away, and so it was with my sister.

God gives us a family to love, honor and respect; we are not to ignore those who he has placed in our lives, or He can take them away. I learned that all souls (life) belong to God (Ezekiel.18: 4), and that He's the final authority when it comes to life and death. A fact made clear as Jesus stood before Pilate who said to him that he, had the power to crucify Jesus or let him live, Jesus' words to him were, he (*Pilate*) had no power at all, except it was given from above (John.19: 11), in other words **NO ONE DIES BEFORE THEIR TIME**.

In his infinite wisdom, the Lord has allowed us to choose where we will spend our eternity when we pass from this life, this is called choice, and free will.

My sister had the light of innocence burning inside her; she was a quiet giver and was not one given to trouble. Ava was very passive and obedient to do what she was asked and more, she was all but invisible apart from the things she did around the house. She had the light of Christ shining from her, but I'm not sure any of us in the house knew it at the time, or just ignored it.

The light was not appreciated until it was taken away and extinguished. When the Lord took Ava home to be with him, it slowly became clear (to me), over the years the life she lived, and although I didn't know it at the time, her death started me moving in the right direction, and that combined with a few other things the Lord had prepared would change my life completely.

It was because of my sister's passing away that I made a promise to myself to always respect women, and although I never hit or put my hands on my sister I did not give her the respect she should have had, she was the only girl in a house full of boys, six in all, and she did not have much of a voice or power to do or say much. She did not complain she would go to her room and occupy herself in her own way quietly.

It's very true what they say, "you don't know what you have until it's gone", my sister lived a full life being here only 11 years, her light burned brightly, and the seeds she planted has grown in my life and has brought forth some amazing memories of her, who she was, as well as manifesting the work, and word of God that would become clearer to me in the years following.

I missed or messed up more than a few opportunities to show my sister how much I loved her, but there is a world filled with women who I can honor her memory with by showing them love and cherishing them as God had intended.

Death is seen more often as violent revenge, a time that is used to get even with someone, a time to be angry or bitter, and display aggression. It's not the same however as we think of someone who is merely sleeping. Sleep is seen as a time of peace, comfort and release. Sleep is not seen as an end but only a time of rest from pain or labor, a time that one will awake feeling and being refreshed, and although my sister is not physically with me, she is always with me.

It was September 1994 when tragedy would again find me, this time when my wife Lora died of cancer. Of course, everyone deals with loss in a personal way depending on the relationship they had with the person who has passed away.

The loss was made more profound as we had children that were young who had now lost their mother, my pain became greater as I thought of our children and what this would mean and do to them.

I had no time to focus on my loss as I had to think of what my children would have to go through and adjust to. You see it was never about me, but about them, and how much I loved them. When loved ones die, it can bring out the best, or the worse in an individual.

Death can be devastating emotionally on everyone, and we'd all wish it did not occur. But it does, and we need to prepare as best we can, for its eventual arrival, and learn to cope with it, and to have our house in order.

I'm sure there are many things we would all do differently if we knew the exact date and time death would come to us.

Did I forget my wife and her sickness, certainly not, but **how we remember a loved one** is just as important as **what we remember about them**?

There might be some measure of comfort for us, if we knew when the sleep of death would come, and we pray it would be peaceful, but this is not the case. Death is often unexpected even when we know it's coming, and the day or the hour is not in our hands to know.

In 1997 my youngest brother Paul would have death pay him a visit; he was an intelligent young man who allowed himself to get caught up in the lures of the world, drugs and a lifestyle that would ultimately lead death to his doorway.

I spent the closing months of his life with him on a daily basis, monitoring the machine he was hooked up to.

He and I spoke of his life and the things he had filled it with. He knew the Lord, but he also heard the call of the world, and followed his flesh, and it took him down a dark road filled with the works of the flesh.

As he lay in the bed sick and unable to do much of anything for himself, he reflected on what brought him to that point. Remarkably he did not blame God or anyone else for his condition only himself.

He said he made his own choices based on what he wanted to do. As a child of God, I was pleased to hear him say he took full responsibility for his own actions (sins). He confessed them, and asked forgiveness, and made as much right as he could before his sleep into eternity.

In the case of my sister Ava, her death came as she was young, and almost suddenly to our family. In the case of my wife she passed away from cancer, and was able to live a longer life but sickness would overtake her, and she passed away, and my brother similarly became sick and finally succumbed to his illness.

Each of their deaths affected me, and impacted me in different ways, and I had a part to play in how I would deal with each of their passing, and to either choose the path of bitterness, or the road that leads to getting and becoming better. I could either place blame on others or make personal change.

Timothy White, Sr.

At some point in time we will all lose a loved one, or might be the loved one lost, but if we prepare our families for our passing from this life, they can, and often will, live a better life knowing we are always with them, in spite of a short time of separation in sleep.

Those who we loved that has passed away are always near us, they are always with us, and that's because we keep them in our hearts. One minute, or 100 years, it's the memories we have and cherish that keeps them alive inside us.

Conclusion

When a human being dies it affects someone somewhere. Screaming, weeping, and mourning, all outward demonstrations of loss, there are those who are believed to have loved greatly because of their tears and those who it is assumed did not love at all because they shed no tears.

Love is not nor should it ever be measured in the amount of tears shed, tears can be anger at God and others, they can be of regret, things that personally could have been done better, and some tears can be of sorrow, the losing of a close friend or member of the family.

How we face this loss depends on one or maybe all the things mentioned above, but as saints of God we should see death differently. We know we cannot avoid it, and as sure as we live, we will one day die, the manner we might not know, or the hour, but we do know The Lord Jesus Christ has conquered death, and made a way for us, and the fear we once had about death has been removed.

We have looked at the power of the resurrection and how death has no power over us in the body of Christ. Weeping is said to endure for a night, but joy comes in the morning.

When our loved ones die in the Lord, it's not time to hang our heads but lift them up.

When will this sadness and loneliness leave us, and how long will it take for this joy to come; when we **stop thinking about our loss and continue to focus on our love**?

About the Author

Timothy White Sr. has impacted thousands of people throughout the world as an author, teacher, motivational speaker and minister. Mr. White is on a mission to positively influence millions of people through his work, ministry and writing, which currently exceeds 80+ books covering a plethora of topics including bullying, domestic violence, self-help, history and spirituality.

The Cleveland, Ohio native, a father of five, has overcome many adversities in his life including homelessness and losing his beloved wife to cancer in 1994. Through much heartache and disappointments he discovered a new purpose and passion to use writing as a tool to "plant positive seeds."

Mr. White has developed profound spiritual insight into relationships over the years. Mr. White has written multiple books on the topic of abuse including, In the Ring with Heels On, She's the Boss and Victims of Bullies. Mr. White writes about these and other issues because of the relevance, and prevalence of domestic and other violence. He believes that, "Information plus application equals transformation."

Mr. White is an Evangelist and former pastor. He believes, "God chooses who He uses." He writes, speaks, and ministers to local, national, and international audiences. With an additional 15 new books in the works, Mr. White hopes to give people plenty of "spiritual food" to eat.

White is one of the producers of the documentary "Where's Gina?" about missing children on which he was also narrator.

He is a co-developer of a tech company (Gsys LLC) that brought blindside technology to vehicles that made billions for the industry, saving countless lives.

He is currently co-hosting a radio show, "Healing the Hurt" on WERE 1490am in Cleveland, Ohio on Thursday evenings 8-10 pm with Host, Rev. Brenda Ware-Abrams.

He is currently on the Advisory Board and is a volunteer instructor at the Juvenile Correction centers in Warrensville Heights and Cleveland, Ohio where his book Seven Signs of Success is being taught.

His book Victims of Bullies is, currently, in the City of Cleveland School system to help stop and make aware of solutions to the issue of bullying.

timwhite55@gmail.com   Timwhitepublishing.com